OWLS

BY MARIA MUDD RUTH

BENCHMARK BOOKS

MARSHALL CAVENDISH
NEW YORK

Series Consultant
James Doherty
General Curator
Bronx Zoo, New York

Thanks to Dr. Christine Sheppard, ornithology curator, Wildlife Conservation Society, Bronx, New York,
for her expert reading of this manuscript.

Benchmark Books
Marshall Cavendish
99 White Plains Road
Tarrytown, NY 10591–9001
www.marshallcavendish.com

Library of Congress Cataloging-in-Publication Data

Ruth, Maria Mudd.
Owls / by Maria Mudd Ruth.
p. cm. – (Animals, animals)
Includes bibliographical references and index.
ISBN 0-7614-1752-4
1. Owls–Juvenile literature. I. Title. II. Series.

QL696.S8M84 2004
598.9'7–dc22
2004000364

Photo Research by Joan Meisel
Cover photo of great gray owl courtesy of *Reuters/Corbis*

Photographs in this book are used by permission and through the courtesy of: *Corbis:* Tim Zurowski, 15; Ron Austing/Frank Lane Picture
Agency, 21-22, 30; Mark Hamblin, 22; Yann Arthus–Bertrand, 23; Joe McDonald, 24, 32; Frank Blackburn/Ecoscene, 26; Lynda Richardson, 31;
Fritz Polking/Frank Lane Picture Agency, 37; Gregory M. Bianchini, 38-39. *Peter Arnold, Inc.:* Carl R. Sams II, 4, 12 (top), 13 (top); Thomas D.
Mangelsen, 8; Martin Harvey, 11, 12 (bottom); Kim Heacox, 12 (center); Tom Vezo, 13(center); C. Allan Morgan, 13(bottom); S.J. Krasemann, 16,
29; Manfred Danegger, 18; Michael Sewell, 34; Bert Gildart, 40.

Printed in China
1 3 5 6 4 2

CONTENTS

1   INTRODUCING OWLS

. . . .   5

2   WHO'S AN OWL?

. . . .   9

3   THE SILENT HUNTERS

. . . .   19

4   LIFE CYCLE

. . . .   27

5   A PROMISING FUTURE?

. . . .   35

GLOSSARY

. . . .   42

FIND OUT MORE

. . . .   44

INDEX

. . . .   46

1
INTRODUCING OWLS

When you think of owls, do you imagine a "wise old owl" staring at you with its large, bright eyes? Do you hear its *hoot hoot hoot* on Halloween night? Do you think an owl can spin its head around and around like a top? Do owls seem scary to you? Do you think owls can be trained to deliver your mail and packages, like Hedwig in the Harry Potter books?

Most of us would answer yes to some of these questions. Most of these ideas, however, are based on stories, cartoons, and movies—not on scientific facts. For example, the idea that owls are wise is thousands of years old. The people of ancient Greece believed owls must be great thinkers because their eyes face forward like ours (not to the side like most birds' eyes) and because they are silent.

THE GREAT HORNED OWL IS ONE OF THE LARGEST AND MOST COMMON OWLS IN NORTH AMERICA. ITS DISTINCTIVE "HORNS" ARE ACTUALLY FEATHERS—NOT HORNS OR EARS.

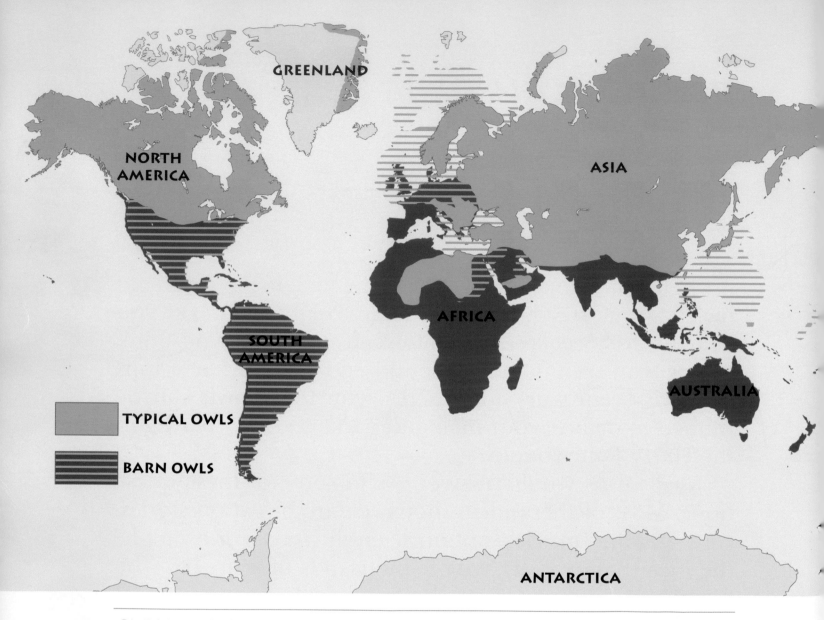

GREENLAND

NORTH
AMERICA

ASIA

SOUTH
AMERICA

AFRICA

AUSTRALIA

TYPICAL OWLS

BARN OWLS

ANTARCTICA

OWLS LIVE IN A WIDE VARIETY OF HABITATS ON NEARLY ALL CONTINENTS OF THE GLOBE. THE MANY SPECIES OF OWLS ARE GROUPED INTO TWO DISTINCT FAMILIES. THE LARGER FAMILY, CALLED TYPICAL OWLS, RANGE WORLDWIDE. MEMBERS OF THE SMALLER GROUP, KNOWN AS BARN OWLS, ARE FOUND IN THE MORE SOUTHERLY AREAS.

In Greek mythology the owl is a symbol of wisdom, and is often seen with Athena, the Greek goddess of wisdom. Owls are certainly smart birds, but scientists believe that parrots, crows, and other birds are probably smarter. Still, schoolchildren today learn the famous poem,

A wise old owl lived in an oak.
The more he saw, the less he spoke.
The less he spoke, the more he heard.
Why can't we all be like that wise old bird?

Most owls are *nocturnal*, or active at night, so they are very difficult to study. In recent years, however, *ornithologists*, the scientists who study birds, have learned much about owls. The facts about real owls in the wild show that their natural behavior is more amazing than any make–believe story or movie about owls.

2
WHO'S AN OWL?

Owls range in size from the tiny elf owl, at about 5.5 inches (14 cm) long, to the great gray owl, at about 2.5 feet (0.76 m) long. Owls live on all continents except Antarctica. They live in many different kinds of places on those continents. These natural places, called *habitats*, have all the living and nonliving things needed for an animal or other organism to survive. The great horned owl and the northern spotted owl, for example, live in the woodland and forest habitats of North America. Spectacled owls live in the tropical rainforest habitats of South America. Most owls live in trees, but burrowing owls live in underground holes in the desert. Snowy owls live in the open spaces of the treeless arctic *tundra*, where the soil is frozen and covered with snow most of the year.

AT HOME ON THE SNOW-COVERED AND TREELESS LAND OF THE TUNDRA, THE SNOWY OWL MAKES ITS NEST ON THE OPEN GROUND. YOUNG BIRDS AND FEMALE BIRDS HAVE FEATHERS WITH DARK BARS AND SPOTS. OLDER MALE SNOWY OWLS MAY BE PURE WHITE.

9

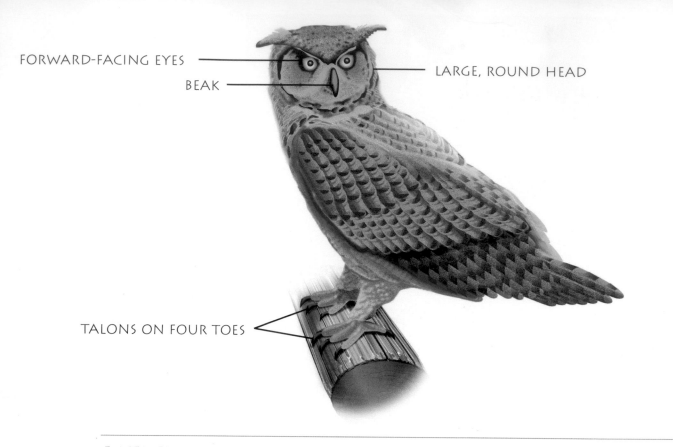

FORWARD-FACING EYES

BEAK

LARGE, ROUND HEAD

TALONS ON FOUR TOES

EXCELLENT VISION AND HEARING, A STRONG BEAK, AND POWERFUL TALONS MAKE THE OWL A FEARSOME PREDATOR.

Owls have special features, called *adaptations*, that help them survive in their specific habitat. These adaptations—such as strong feet; sharp, curved claws, called *talons*; unusual eyes; and large, fuzzy feathers covering their flight feathers—help make owls successful *predators*, or animals that hunt and eat other animals. Birds that are predators are also called *raptors*. The wide variety of animals that owls hunt, called *prey*, include small mammals, birds, reptiles, amphibians, fish, and insects. An owl's powerful feet help it grasp and hold prey. Each foot has four forward-facing toes that end in sharp, flesh-piercing talons.

An owl's forward-facing eyes allow for *binocular vision.* This kind of vision allows an owl to focus both eyes on a single object. Binocular vision improves an owl's ability to judge how close or far away an object is. This helps the owl to hunt swiftly moving prey. An owl's tubular-shaped eyes are much more sensitive to light than human eyes. This is important because most owls are nocturnal.

THE EYES OF A PREDATOR MAY BE ITS MOST POWERFUL TOOLS. OWLS HAVE UNUSUAL TUBULAR-SHAPED EYEBALLS THAT ARE EXTREMELY SENSITIVE TO LIGHT. SEEING WELL IN THE DARK AND IN LOW LIGHT IS IMPORTANT FOR NOCTURNAL HUNTERS.

OWL SPECIES

HERE ARE SIX OWL SPECIES WITH APPROXIMATE ADULT WEIGHT, LENGTH (HEAD TO TOE), AND WINGSPAN.

Great Gray Owl
27 inches (68.6 cm) long
2.4 pounds (1 kg)
52-inch (1.32-m) wingspan

Great Horned Owl
22 inches (56 cm) long
3.1 pounds (1.4 kg)
44-inch (1.1-m) wingspan

Malay Fish Owl
18 inches (46 cm) long
2.8 pounds (1.2 kg)
14-inch (35.5-cm) wingspan

Burrowing Owl
9.5 inches (24 cm) long
5 ounces (141.7 g)
21-inch (53-cm) wingspan

Eastern Screech Owl
8.5 inches (21.6 cm) long
6 ounces (170 g)
20-inch (51-cm) wingspan

Elf Owl
5.8 inches (14.7 cm) long
1.4 ounces (39.7 g)
13-inch (33-cm) wingspan

Because of the large size and tubular shape of its eyeballs, the owl has no extra room in its skull for the muscles needed to move its eyes in their sockets. The eyes cannot move to the left or right, so the owl always directs its eyes straight ahead. To see in other directions, the owl relies on the fourteen vertebrae in its neck (most mammals, including giraffes, only have seven), which allow it to turn its head around and face backward or even upside-down. Some television cartoons show owls spinning their heads around and around. Careful observation shows that an owl can turn its head about 270 degrees—about three-quarters of a full circle. Starting with its head looking over one shoulder, it can turn to face forward, then continue turning to face directly behind it. Sometimes an owl turns its head so rapidly that it appears to be spinning.

Owls have extremely sensitive hearing. Though the tufts of feathers on top of some owls' heads look like ears, they are not. An owl's ears are openings located on the side of its head. These openings are well hidden behind the circles of feathers, called *facial disks*, around an owl's eyes. The disks help funnel sounds toward the ear openings.

Most owls have a blend of brown, black, white, and

THE TUFTS OF FEATHERS ATOP AN OWL'S HEAD ARE NOT EARS. THE EAR OPENINGS ARE LOCATED ON THE SIDES OF THE HEAD AND ARE HIDDEN BY FACIAL DISK FEATHERS.

EXCEPT FOR ITS BRIGHTLY COLORED EYES AND FEET, THIS WESTERN SCREECH OWL IS VERY WELL CAMOUFLAGED IN THE FOREST WHERE IT LIVES. BARK-COLORED PLUMAGE HELPS KEEP THIS SMALL OWL HIDDEN FROM BOTH ITS PREDATORS AND ITS PREY.

gray feathers. These shadowy colors *camouflage* the owls, or disguise them, so they blend in with the color of their background. When they are in the forest against a back–ground of trees and bark, owls are almost impossible to spot. The adult snowy owl's pure white feathers camouflage it in the snowy winter tundra.

3
THE SILENT HUNTERS

Owls are known as the silent hunters. Unlike other raptors, owls have wings covered with velvety feathers and front wing feathers with edges that look like a comb. These unique features help muffle the sound of the air whooshing over an owl's wings as it flies.

When hunting, owls are all eyes and ears. They sit on an elevated perch, such as a tree branch or fence post, in an upright position. They watch and listen for the telltale squeak of a mouse, the flash of a grasshopper, or the crunching of dry leaves beneath tiny paws. The owl turns to pinpoint the sound or movement. When the prey is within striking range, the owl swoops down on silent wings. It swings its powerful feet forward to grasp the prey in its talons, flying back up to a tree limb to eat it whole, or in small pieces if the prey is large.

ON SILENT, VELVETY-SOFT WINGS, THIS BARN OWL MAY BE MAKING NIGHTTIME LANDING IN THE WOODS OR A STEALTHY ATTACK ON AN UNSUSPECTING PREY.

A SAW-WHET OWL SWOOPS DOWN
ON A WHITE-FOOTED MOUSE.

A BURROWING OWL FEASTS ON AN ANOLE LIZARD.

Several hours after eating, an owl coughs up a *pellet*, a compressed wad of bones, fur, scales, or feathers that it cannot digest. Scientists take these pellets apart and put the bones back together to learn about an owl's diet.

4
LIFE CYCLE

Being a skilled hunter is especially important for male owls during spring courtship. During this time, he must prove to a female that he can provide enough food for her and their future owlets. The males hunt and show off what they catch to available females. Some males will show off how well they fly by making spectacular swooping flights and even passing food to females in flight! If a female is impressed, the pair will nest together.

Owls use nests but rarely build them. Many owls nest in natural cavities or holes that were built by other birds such as woodpeckers. Owls too large for cavities use the open-air nests of birds such as crows and red-tailed hawks. The owls may use an abandoned nest or chase the nest-building bird away.

A LONG-EARED OWL SITS WITH ITS CHICKS IN A NEST MADE OF STICKS. OWLS RARELY BUILD THEIR OWN NESTS, SO THIS ONE PROBABLY BELONGED TO A CROW, HAWK, MAGPIE, OR OTHER BIRD.

In the desert, the burrowing owl uses the underground holes and tunnels dug by prairie dogs, gophers, ground squirrels, armadillos, or skunks. If the burrowing owl cannot find a suitable burrow, it may use its talons and extra long legs to dig its own. Burrowing owls protect their burrows by lining them with animal dung. The scent of the dung may disguise the owl's scent and keep predators away. If a predator enters the burrow, this clever owl may make a noise that imitates the sound of a rattlesnake's tail.

Wherever they are, owl nests are safe places to lay eggs and raise owlets. Owls lay from two to sixteen eggs, depending on the species of owl and the health of the female. If prey is abundant, the female will lay more eggs. If prey is scarce, she will lay only a few eggs or none at all.

An owl does not lay its eggs all at once, but at intervals of at least a day and up to three days apart. For about one month the female *incubates* the eggs, or sits on them to warm them with her body heat so they hatch. When the chicks hatch, the father brings prey to the nest and the mother shreds it into small pieces for the chicks. The chicks stay on the nest for a few months and learn to fly and hunt. When the young owls are old enough, they leave their parents' nest to establish their own territory.

THE BURROWING OWL IS THE ONLY NORTH AMERICAN OWL THAT NESTS IN UNDERGROUND BURROWS UP TO 10 FEET (3 M) LONG. THESE OWLS INHABIT OPEN COUNTRY WHERE THEY HUNT BY DAY.

DON'T EXPECT THESE YOUNG SCREECH OWLS TO SCREECH. EVEN ON HALLOWEEN.
THIS OWL SPECIES HAS A CALL THAT SOUNDS LIKE A TREMBLING WHISTLE. MOST
OWL SPECIES USE DIFFERENT CALLS FOR ATTRACTING MATES OR DEFENDING
THEIR TERRITORY.

Some owls stay close to their parents' territory, but others fly great distances. Barn owls occasionally travel more than 1,000 miles (1,600 km) away from their first nest!

When a young male owl establishes its hunting territory, it can be quite noisy as it hoots back and forth with other owls during the night. Because the hooting takes place in the autumn, pictures and stories of owls have become part of Halloween celebrations.

Some owls call in a steady *hoot hoot hoot*, but owls also use a great variety of rhythms and combinations of long

THESE FLUFFY GREAT HORNED OWL CHICKS MAY SPEND UP TO THREE MONTHS IN THE CARE OF THEIR PARENTS BEFORE THEY ARE READY TO FLY OFF ON THEIR OWN.

and short hoots to communicate. The great horned owl, for instance, has a deep *ho hoo hoo hoododo hoooo hoo*. The barred owl's hoots sound like someone is asking, "Who cooks for YOU? Who cooks for YOU all?"

THREE-MONTH-OLD EASTERN SCREECH OWL FLEDGLINGS.

The great horned owl also makes a loud call that sounds like a barking dog. The barred owl makes barking, cackling, and gurgling notes. When alarmed, a female snowy owl makes a quacking sound. The screech owl does not actually screech. It makes trembling calls and hollow whistles that run up and down the musical scale. It is the barn owl that calls a long, hissing shriek or screech.

5
A PROMISING FUTURE?

Over the years, scientists have learned many things about the mysterious owl, including the fact that it can be helpful to people.

Owls play an important role in the balance of nature. The populations of many varieties of animals and insects would grow out of control if owls and other predators did not hunt them. Many of these animals and insects are considered pests by people–especially farmers, who lose tons of stored grain and crops each year to rodents, rabbits, and insects. Barn owls may eat as many as three mice a night–that's a thousand a year!

And yet humans have been responsible for great declines in owl populations. The main reason for this is that as the human population grows, it takes over more of the

POPULATIONS OF THE NORTHERN SPOTTED OWL HAVE BEEN DIMINISHING RAPIDLY AS THE TREES THEY NEST IN HAVE BEEN CUT DOWN AND THE FORESTS WHERE THEY LIVE AND HUNT HAVE BEEN DESTROYED.

land where owls live and nest. By cutting down forests and plowing up prairies to build highways, homes, offices, schools, or other buildings, people force owls to live in smaller territories, with fewer prey and more competition from other owls and birds.

In the United States, the ancient forests of the Pacific Northwest have been heavily logged for lumber and the spotted owls that live there are at risk of becoming extinct. In some parts of the United States and Canada, some burrowing owl populations have declined because the animals that dig the burrows that the owls live in– the prairie dogs–have been killed and their burrows plowed over to create land for farming.

If people make thoughtful and wise choices, perhaps these owls can be saved from extinction. Many owls, such as the northern spotted owl and the burrowing owl, have been placed on lists of threatened and endangered animals. These owls and their habitats get special protection, which may help them survive. In most places, hunting owls is illegal and only people with special scientific permits can capture or keep an owl for research studies.

While growing human populations may endanger some owls, it seems to be helping others. Some screech

PLACES WHERE BURROWING OWLS CAN LIVE AND RAISE THEIR OWLETS HAVE BECOME FEWER AND FEWER OVER THE YEARS AS THE OPEN LAND THEY NEED IS CONVERTED TO FARMLAND, HIGHWAYS, AND HOUSING DEVELOPMENTS.

owls living in suburban neighborhoods where large trees grow may actually live longer than the screech owls living in the countryside. There are fewer predators in the suburbs and more prey, such as small birds and rodents attracted to backyard bird feeders and garbage cans.

THIS SCREECH OWL HAS TAKEN
UP RESIDENCE IN A MAN-MADE
NESTING BOX.

FINDING A HOME, FOOD, AND MATE HAS BECOME MORE DIFFICULT FOR OWLS, INCLUDING THIS NORTHERN SAW-WHET OWL. AS THE HUMAN POPULATION GROWS, THERE IS LESS AND LESS HABITAT FOR THESE AND OTHER CREATURES.

Scientists are learning that some owls can change their habits as their environments change. Spotted owls, once believed to nest only in dense forests of trees more than two hundred years old, are able to nest in much younger trees growing in small patches of forest. Many owls that normally nest in natural cavities in trees will use nest boxes if natural cavities are not available. Nest boxes are simple man-made wooden boxes built for owls large and small. When they are placed within or near the owl's natural habitat, they make safe places for owls to lay their eggs and raise their owlets. Though these owls can survive and reproduce in these habitats, scientists are not certain if young forests or nest boxes can guarantee a healthy population. By preserving their natural habitats and by studying these fascinating birds, we can be as wise as the owl.

adaptations: Special features that help an animal survive in its habitat.

binocular vision: Vision that uses both eyes to focus on a single object.

camouflage: To disguise something so it blends in with the color of its background.

facial disks: The circles of feathers around an owl's eyes that help funnel sounds toward the ear openings.

habitats: Places that have all the living and non-living things an animal or other organism needs to survive.

incubates: Sits on eggs to warm them with body heat so they hatch.

nocturnal: Active at night.

ornithologists: Scientists that study birds.

pellet: A wad of coughed up bones, beaks, fur, and other animal parts an owl cannot digest.

predators: Animals that hunt other animals for food.

prey: An animal that is hunted and eaten by a predator.

raptors: Birds that hunt other animals for food; another name for birds of prey.

talons: The sharp, curved claws of many birds of prey.

tundra: A treeless land, usually above the Arctic Circle, where the soil is frozen most of the year.

F I N D   O U T   M O R E

BOOKS

National Audubon Society *Pocket Guide to North American Birds of Prey.* New York: Knopf, 1994.

Price, Ann. *Raptors: The Eagles, Hawks, Falcons, and Owls of North America.* Lanham, MD: Roberts Rinehart, 2002.

Shedd, Warner. *Owls Aren't Wise & Bats Aren't Blind: A Naturalist Debunks Our Favorite Fallacies About Wildlife.* New York: Crown, 1994.

Sutton, Patricia Taylor. *How to Spot an Owl.* Boston: Houghton Mifflin, 1999.

WEB SITES

North and Central American Owls
www.owling.com

Northern Barred Owl Family in Action
www.owlcam.com

The Owl Pages
www.owlpages.com

World Owl Trust
www.owls.org

ABOUT THE AUTHOR

Maria Mudd Ruth is the author of several natural history books for young adults, including *Hawks and Falcons, Snakes, The Deserts of the Southwest, The Mississippi River, The Pacific Coast, The Tundra* (all Benchmark Book titles), and *The Ultimate Ocean Book.* She is currently writing a book for adults on a mysterious seabird of the Pacific Coast.

INDEX

Page numbers for illustrations are in **boldface.**

maps
range, **6**

adaptations, 10, **10, 16,** 17, 19, 23
   to habitat loss, 36–41

barn owls, **6, 22,** 31, 33, 35
burrowing owls, 13, **13, 24,** 28, 36, **37**

chicks, 28, **31**
claws. *See* talons
colors, **8, 16,** 17
communication, 31
conservation, **38–39,** 41
courtship, 27

days and nights, 7, **11,** 11, 23
defenses, 28
   camouflage, **16,** 17
digestion, 25

eastern screech owl, 13, **13**
eating, 19, 35
ecology, 35
eggs, 28

elf owl, 9, 13, **13**
eyes, 5, **11,** 11, 14

facial disks, 14, **15,** 23
feathers
   as adaptation, 10
   colors, **16,** 17
   on head, **4, 8,** 14, **15**
   of snowy owls, **8,** 9
   on wings, 19
feet, **10,** 10–11, 19
females, 28
fish owls, 12, **12,** 23, **23**
flying, **18,** 19, **20–21,** 27

geographic distribution, **6,** 9
great gray owl, 12, **12**
great horned owl, **4,** 9, 12, **12,** 22, **31,** 33
Greek mythology, 5, 7

habitats, **6,** 9, 36–37, **37**
   changing, 36–41
   loss, 35–36, **37, 40**
Halloween, 5, 31
head, 14, **15,** 19, 23
hearing, 14, 19, 23
horns, **4**

human beings, 35–37, **38–39,** 41
hunting, 10–11, **18,** 19, **20–21,** 23, 27

intelligence, 5, 7

life span, 36–37
long-eared owls, **26**

males, 27, 28, 31

nests, **26,** 27–28, **29, 38–39,** 41
North America, 9, 36

parenting, 28, **37**
poem, 7
predators, 28, 37
prey, 10, 19, **20–21, 22,** 22–23, **24,** 28, 35, 36, 37

raptors, 10
reproduction, 28, 41

saw-whet owls, **20–21, 40**
screech owls, 13, **13, 16, 30,** 33, 36–37, **38–39**

sight, 11, **11,** 14, 19
sizes, 9, 12–13
snowy owls, **8,** 9, 17, 33
sounds, 5, 28, **30,** 31–33
South America, 9
species, **12,** 12–13, **13**
   endangered or threatened, **34,** 35–36, **37, 40**
spectacled owls, 9
spotted owls, 9, **34,** 41

talons, **10,** 10–11, 19
territoriality, 28, 31
travel, 28–31
typical owls, **6**

Web sites, 44
wings, **18,** 19